REPTILES

PREDATORS

Written by
Mignonne Gunasekara

BookLife
PUBLISHING

©2020
BookLife Publishing Ltd.
King's Lynn
Norfolk PE30 4LS

ISBN: 978-1-83927-259-2

Written by:
Mignonne Gunasekara

Edited by:
Shalini Vallepur

Designed by:
Gareth Liddington

A catalogue record for this book is available from the British Library.

All facts, statistics, web addresses and URLs in this book were verified as valid and accurate at time of writing. No responsibility for any changes to external websites or references can be accepted by either the author or publisher.

All rights reserved.
Printed in Malaysia.

CONTENTS

Page 4	Meet the Predators
Page 6	Gila Monster
Page 8	Alligator Snapping Turtle
Page 10	King Cobra
Page 12	Central Bearded Dragon
Page 14	Green Anaconda
Page 16	Komodo Dragon
Page 18	Reticulated Python
Page 20	Nile Crocodile
Page 22	Weight a Minute
Page 24	Glossary and Index

Words that look like <u>this</u> can be found in the glossary on page 24.

MEET THE PREDATORS

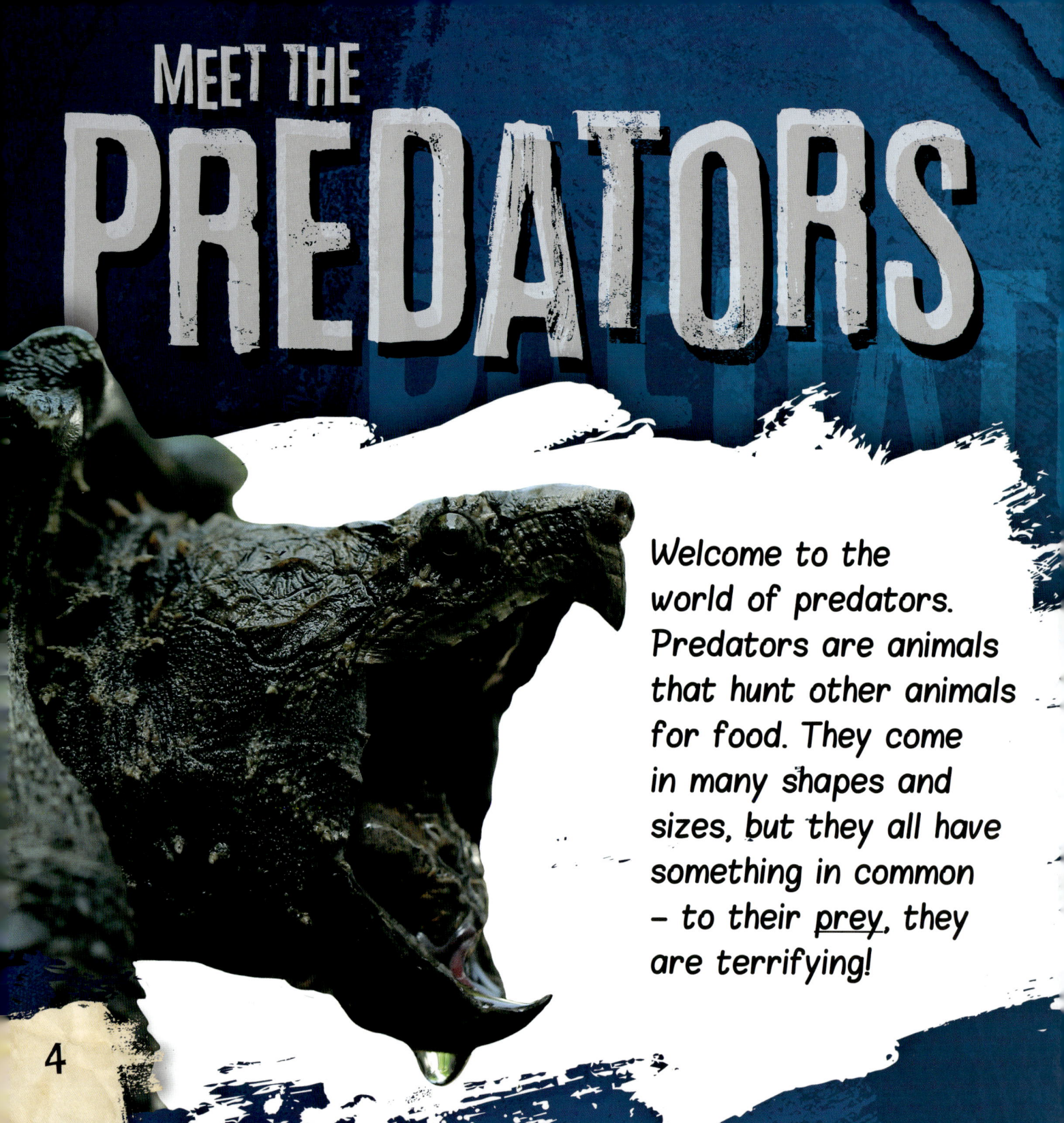

Welcome to the world of predators. Predators are animals that hunt other animals for food. They come in many shapes and sizes, but they all have something in common – to their <u>prey</u>, they are terrifying!

Cold-blooded animals have blood that changes temperature with the temperature around them.

In this book, we will be looking at predators that are reptiles. Reptiles are scaly, cold-blooded animals that usually have a backbone.

GILA MONSTER

Gila monsters are <u>venomous</u>. They sometimes chew while biting an animal to get their venom deep into the bite and into the animal's blood.

Gila monsters steal eggs from other animals' nests and eat them.

Fat stored in a Gila monster's tail and body can keep it going when it hasn't eaten in a long time. This is useful because Gila monsters spend most of their lives underground.

Fact File

Habitat: Desert

Weapons: Venom

Prey: Eggs, small birds, frogs, small mammals, insects, carrion

ALLIGATOR SNAPPING TURTLE

Alligator snapping turtles are some of the largest turtles in the world. They hunt for prey using a lure that looks like a worm.

Lure

Alligator snapping turtles spend most of their lives in water.

An alligator snapping turtle sits still and wiggles the red lure on its tongue. When prey gets close to have a look, the turtle snaps its mouth shut and eats it.

Fact File

Habitat: Rivers and lakes in the US

Weapons: Lure, snapping bite

Prey: Fish, frogs

KING COBRA

King cobras can lift the front part of their bodies off the ground and keep moving forward. They do this to scare away animals that are scaring them.

Hood

King cobras spread out their hoods and hiss when scared.

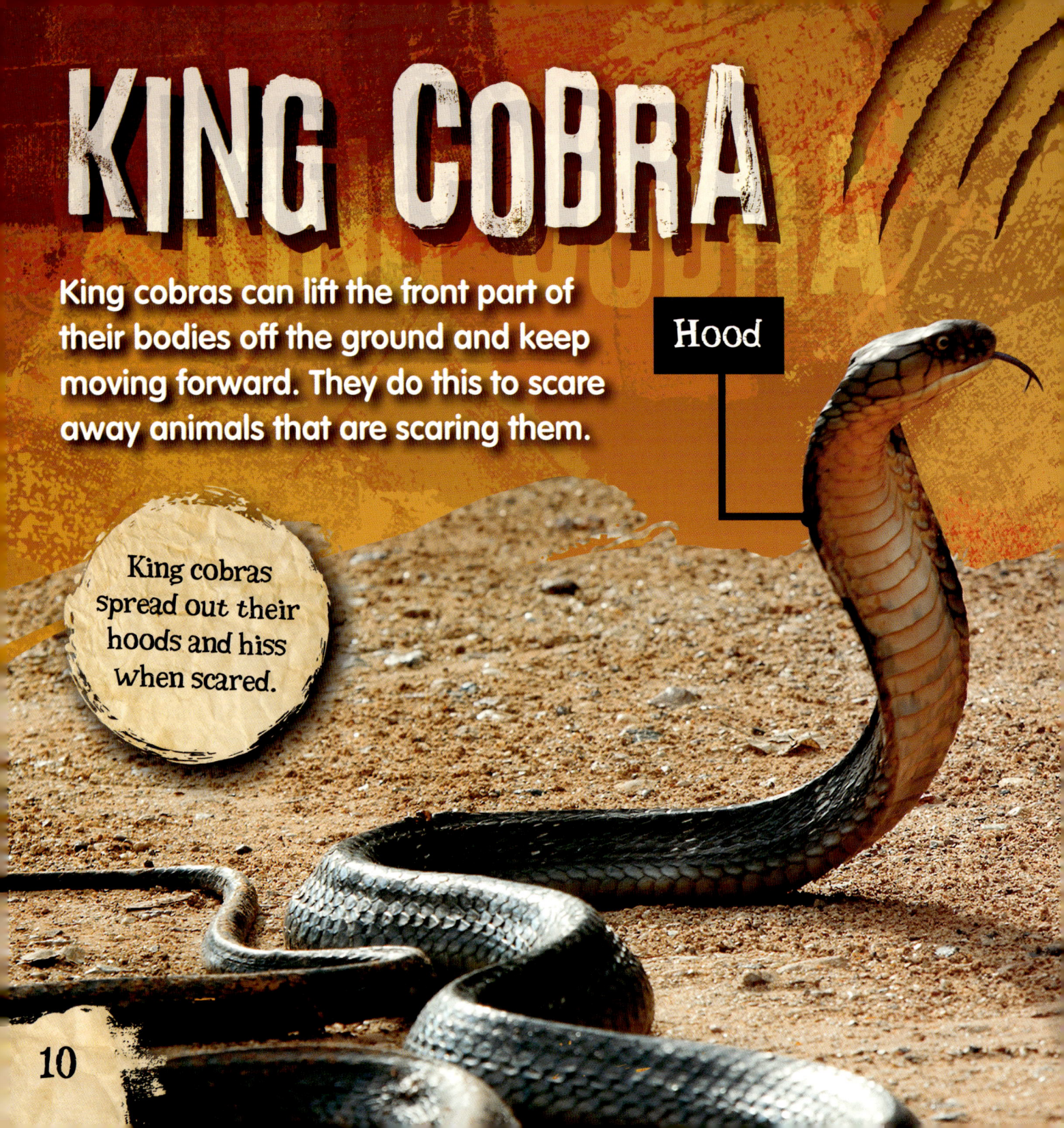

The king cobra is the longest venomous snake in the world. It can climb trees and swim. Its main prey is other snakes.

Fact File

Habitat: Forests in south Asia and southeast Asia

Weapons: Fangs, venom

Prey: Other snakes, small mammals, lizards

The venom from one king cobra bite can kill an elephant.

CENTRAL BEARDED DRAGON

A central bearded dragon's beard is made of spiky scales around its chin. Bearded dragons come from Australia, where they live in warm, dry habitats.

Bearded dragons can puff up their beards to look scarier to attackers.

Central bearded dragons are omnivores, which means they eat meat and plants. They are good climbers and have been seen sitting on fence posts and tree branches.

Fact File

Habitat: Desert, woodland

Weapons: Strong bite, sticky tongue

Prey: Insects, small lizards

GREEN ANACONDA

Green anacondas are constrictors. This means they kill their prey by wrapping their strong bodies around it and squeezing tight. The prey dies because it can't breathe.

The green anaconda is the heaviest snake in the world.

Green anacondas can open their mouths really wide to swallow prey whole. They can survive without eating for weeks or months after a big meal.

Green anacondas are good swimmers and often hunt in water.

Fact File

Habitat: <u>Swamps</u>, <u>marshes</u> and slow-moving waters in South America

Weapons: Strong body, good swimmer

Prey: Mammals, birds, fish, reptiles

15

KOMODO DRAGON

Komodo dragons will eat whatever prey they can find. They eat carrion but also hunt large animals such as deer and water buffalo.

Forked tongue

The Komodo dragon is the largest lizard in the world.

Komodo dragons wait for prey to come close to them before attacking. If prey gets away, Komodo dragons will follow it until it dies, then eat it.

Fact File

Habitat: Hot island forests or <u>savannahs</u> in Indonesia

Weapons: Claws, teeth, spit

Prey: Carrion, deer, pigs, smaller Komodo dragons

A Komodo dragon's spit is thought to be deadly.

RETICULATED PYTHON

The reticulated python is the longest snake in the world.

Reticulated pythons can climb trees in the forests they call home. They are also good swimmers and can often be found in or near water.

Like green anacondas, reticulated pythons are also constrictors.

Reticulated pythons eat mammals such as large deer or pigs. They can <u>sense</u> heat, which helps them find prey hiding in leaves or in the dark.

Fact File

Habitat: Warm forests in southeast Asia

Weapons: Good swimmer, strong body, can sense heat

Prey: Birds, mammals

NILE CROCODILE

Adult Nile crocodiles are apex predators. This means they don't have any predators themselves. Nile crocodiles are known to eat whatever prey they can find.

Sharp teeth

Baby Nile crocodiles eat small prey, such as insects.

Nile crocodiles even eat spiky porcupines, small hippos and zebras. They also eat carrion and have been known to attack humans that get too close to them.

Nile crocodiles can eat prey as large as wildebeest.

Fact File

Habitat: Rivers, swamps and marshes in Africa

Weapons: Strength, sharp teeth

Prey: Birds, reptiles, mammals

WEIGHT A MINUTE

Congratulations, you met the predators! Weren't they fierce? Some of them get pretty heavy too. Let's see how much these reptiles can weigh!

Komodo dragon

Up to 900 kilograms

Nile crocodile

Around 135 kilograms

Around 9 kilograms
Alligator snapping turtle

Around 227 kilograms

Which reptile can weigh the most?

King cobra

Up to 100 kilograms

Green anaconda